Psalm

CW00860057

Power of the 23rd Psalm, the Lord is my Shepherd and Your Provisions

Pius Joseph © Text 2020

or other electronic or mechanical methods, without the prior written permission of the publisher

Except in the case of brief quotations embodied in critical reviews and certain other noncommercial uses permitted by copyright law.

The author is aware that the application of this book may differ from one person to another as such things as faith, persistence, trust, and love for God can determine the outcomes that you receive from the application of the principles in this book.

TABLE OF CONTENTS

CHAPTER 1

Shepherd

Psalm 23:1

The Lord is my shepherd;

When David got the inspiration to pen down the contents of this scripture as inspired by the Holy Spirit, he was shepherding the flocks of his father. While his brothers who cared nothing about him or the father's business were at home. It never bothered them that a little boy who should be at home was rather in the bush taking care of the sheep, exposed to the danger of being torn apart by wild beasts of the field. No wonder when David came to the battlefield, the only thing that bothered his careless elder brother, Eliab was with who have you left these few sheep in the wilderness (1 Samuel 17:28).

David has seen how he took care of the sheep. Day and night, he was there for the sheep because he knows that if he leaves the sheep for a single moment, the wild beast would invade the sheep and scatter them. Even when he sleeps at night, it won't be deep. His one eye is opened, while the other is closed. And when he perceived an unusual noise among the sheep, he wakes to check what was happening. He passes the sheep through different pasture fields.

And if David can put his life on the line so that the sheep can be satisfied, then God can do much better.

Jesus said I am the good shepherd.

John 10:11

> *I am the good shepherd: the good shepherd giveth his life for the sheep.*

The scriptural reference shows us that Jesus is a good shepherd to all of his children. But before you enjoy his shepherding, you must become a sheep. If you aren't a sheep, he can't be your shepherd. This is where the first big question lies. The Bible uses the word Sheep for a good reason. You need to see how the shepherds in the wilderness tend to their sheep. And sheep are some of the animals that will go where ever the shepherd wants them to. It is only the sheep that are qualified for his shepherding.

I love the way the Holy Spirit inspired David to write this scripture here. It was well arranged so that the Lord must be your shepherd first before proceeding to other vital areas of our consideration in the subsequent chapters.

3

In case you are reading this right now and you aren't his sheep, it is never too late to be one. You can submit your life to him and become his sheep. A simple prayer will satisfy the shepherding requirement:

> *Lord Jesus, I come before you today and I'm asking you to forgive me my sins and cleanse me from all unrighteousness. Write my name in the book of life and give me the grace to serve you forever in Jesus name. Amen*

Reflection

Isaiah 40:11

> *He shall feed his flock like a shepherd: he shall gather the lambs with his arm, and carry them in his bosom, and shall gently lead those that are with young.*

John 10:11

> *I am the good shepherd: the good shepherd giveth his life for the sheep.*

Holy Father, I want to thank you for the privilege that you have given me to become your sheep. To you be all the glory in the name of Jesus.

Heavenly Father, as I submit myself to the leading of the shepherd, I will enjoy all the benefits of being your sheep in the name of Jesus.

Gracious Father, you have said in your word that nothing shall be able to pluck me out of your hands. As your shepherd, I will forever remain under your powerful hands in the name of Jesus.

CHAPTER 2

Wanting

Psalms 23:1

> *I shall not want.*

Even though the Lord is the shepherd of many of us, the wanting we experience can be very diverse. From the daily cares of the things that we need for our lives, to the want of health, and wanting in many other areas of the life of a child of God. When a believer is constantly living in want either of daily needs or even of his needs of life, it is either he has not fully comprehended the role of the shepherd in his life or he has failed to rest in the arms of the shepherd and watch his needs met and his wants satisfied.

When a shepherd is guiding the sheep, the sheep don't worry about where to find the pastures necessary for the sustenance of their daily needs. The sheep know that as long as they are in the care of the shepherd, their pastures for the day are going to be fully provided. And that is where many a believer has a problem. They are aware of the fact that the Lord is their shepherd but haven't been able to find rest in the shepherd's arms. Never will a sheep worry about what to eat. They know that the shepherd will guide them to where their food for the day is located.

The shepherd, being wise knows the spot where to take the sheep for pastures. How our needs are to be met by the shepherd should never be a source of concern to us. He knows where to take us to find our green pastures. Even in the face of raging drought, he will gingerly take the sheep to where they will feed.

For believers, we need to be fully aware that the shepherd role of Jesus in our lives is the same. The believer is called upon to trust him to where his wants and his needs would be fully met. Just as the sheep are taken to where their daily pastures are, that is how God leads us to where our wants are to be met. For some people, the shepherd will lead them to a business to carry out. Through that business, all their financial blessings are satisfied there. It could be a job or even something that looks small. The Bible tells us that he uses the foolish things of this world to confirm the wise. The problem is when the shepherd shows some of us where our pastures are, we are quick to disdain it. We think that well, I want to start making a thousand dollars every day so why should I begin small.

Friends, if you are a faithful sheep, you won't be bothered by where the shepherd is taking you for satisfaction. The challenge is when the shepherd shows us where our needs are to be met, we cower in discouragement when what he has shown us doesn't produce the quickest results. The Bible tells us that whatever is born of God overcomes the world.

1 John 3:9

> *Whosoever is born of God doth not commit sin; for his seed remaineth in him: and he cannot sin, because he is born of God.*

If the business or anything that we do originates from God and not what we conceived and then run to the shepherd to endorse the seal of his blessings upon it, then it must surely overcome. It will grow to the point that it will not only be a blessing to us but to others around us. This is where the problem of many believers lies. The shepherd has been showing them where to feed, but they are insisting on feeding somewhere else, a pasture where he did not take them to.

The shepherd has a personal relationship with each of the sheep he leads to the pasture where they will be satisfied. Where the shepherd will guide sheep *"A"* for his pasture will not be the same place where he would take sheep "**B**" for his pasture. Which is the reason why no believer should compete with another. Where your pasture is located, may not be the same as that of another. The shepherd will guide you to where yours is, provided that you are willing to feed in the place where he has taken you. The shepherd is an expert in that area who knows the places where the pastures are the greenest. But when we begin to do a particular business because we saw that an individual is succeeding in that business, we will not be able to have the grace to succeed in it. The shepherd is not leading us rather we are choosing to feed on that pasture based on what we can see. This constitutes one of the strongest reasons why believers struggle to have their needs met and satisfied. When we decide to take ourselves to the place where the shepherd hasn't taken us to, we will lose his shepherd guide and a life of struggle begins to set in. Poverty, lack, and want become the order of the day. Why? The sheep are feeding on the pasture that the shepherd hasn't led him to.

In 2015, I authored my first ever Christian book, The Vision from the Heavenly. This book was published on Amazon. I then wrote another book, The Baptism of the Holy Spirit. The book was such a blessing to the lives of many that I began to receive emails from people around the world how the book has touched or changed their lives. In the midst of that, I was writing a lot of secular books on different subject matter. My goal for writing the secular books was to make money at least to be able to satisfy my wants. My friend and brother in the Lord, Pastor Daniel, read the book the baptism of the Holy Spirit and was blessed by the message the Lord gave me in the book. He urged me to begin to write Christian books because he saw that it will be a blessing to the life of many. In his words, "whenever you see anything that is inspired by the Holy Spirit, you will know."

But the lure of the little money I was making while writing secular books did not allow me to listen to this wise counsel of the servant of God. I continued writing these books until when it became so overwhelming that God wanted me to start writing Christian books fully. That is where my pasture is located. And through it, my needs will be fully met. I may not be making all the money that I wanted from my Christian books, but I'm fully aware that financial blessings would come later. And I also know that, besides the book blessing the lives of many people who my voice couldn't have reached, it will also bless me too because I learn from what I write.

It doesn't matter where the shepherd is taking you to for your pasture. What is important is that the shepherd is showing you where to feed. I have never seen where a shepherd takes his sheep to a pasture where they will eat and die.

In the same vein, whenever the shepherd is leading you to your pasture, that place is holding your money or financial blessing. Some people's pasture is on the Internet. Others may be in a little business here and there. While some, in a job that the shepherd leads them to. It is important to know that it is the shepherd that is showing you what to do to have your needs satisfied. When we struggle with our needs, is because we do not understand what the shepherd is showing us.

I know that as you are reading this right now, the Holy Spirit is beginning to minister to your heart some of the things that God has shown you in the past that would have turned around your financial struggles. You disregarded that leading of the shepherd which is the reason for your struggle today. If that is your case, I pray that the Lord will show you mercy by taking you to a different pasture or to the same one he has shown you before.

Beyond the desire to satisfy our wants financially, the believer can also be wanting in many other areas of life. A believer can also want in health. A believer can also want in his marriage. When the Bible says the Lord is my shepherd, I shall not want is referring to a situation where a believer can enjoy the complete and total package of salvation. He should not have money, while his marriage is in shambles. He should not also have money, while his health is standing on rickety feet. It must be a complete and total package that the believer can enjoy. He should never want in any area of his life. That is what the Bible means by, "*I shall not want*". When a believer is beginning to want in any area of his life, it is either he has not comprehended the role of the shepherd in his life or he doesn't know how to appropriate the words of the shepherd into his life for his pasture. This is very essential for us to know because when the Bible says the Lord is my shepherd and I shall not want, is far beyond financial needs alone. It goes into the core of the salvation of that believer.

Friends, is there any area of your life that you are wanting? Maybe yours may be in health. Or it may not even be in your health, it may be in your relationship with your kids. It can also be at your job that everything seems to be turning against you and the way you are seeing things, it may lead to losing your job.

I want you to take away the cap of limitation that has been placed on the Scripture as a result of the many preaching that some of us have heard. No matter the interpretation of Scripture that has been painted in our hearts, the truth of the word of God stands sure. That God wants to have total believers on the face of the earth because he knows that it is possible for the totality of the lives which the children of God enjoy to be a source of ministration to those who are around them.

If you have been struggling with any area of your life, I want to let you know that the Lord is about to visit you right now in the name of Jesus.

Scripture for Meditation

John 10:11

> *I am the good shepherd: the good shepherd giveth his life for the sheep.*

Prayers

Reflection

1 Peter 2:25

> *For ye were as sheep going astray; but are now returned unto the Shepherd and Bishop of your souls.*

Philippians 4:19

But my God shall supply all your need according to his riches in glory by Christ Jesus.

Righteous Father, I want to thank you for the privilege of being your sheep and for deciding to come and die on the cross of Calvary so that you can shepherd my life to you be all the glory and honour in the name of Jesus.

Holy Father, I come before you today to ask for mercy where you have shown me my pasture and I have refused to feed there, I pray for your forgiveness in the name of Jesus.

Heavenly Father, now that I have received your forgiveness concerning feeding on the pasture that you haven't led me to, I pray that you will show me where I need to feed so that my wants will be fully satisfied in the name of Jesus.

Gracious Father, I ask for the revelation of the green pastures that will change my financial situation in the name of Jesus.

Righteous Father, let the power of the Scripture that says in the book of Psalms 23, that I shall not want be activated over my life in the name of Jesus.

Gracious Father, by the power of that same Scripture, let every want, lack, and poverty be broken off my life in the name of Jesus.

Holy Father, today I terminate every want over my marriage in the name of Jesus.

Heavenly Father, today I terminate every want over my finances in the name of Jesus.

Holy Father, today I terminate every want over my health in the name of Jesus.

Heavenly Father, today I terminate every want in all areas of my life that the expression of want is showing itself in the name of Jesus.

Gracious Father, I pray that from today henceforth I will begin to enjoy the total package of being a believer that is devoid of want in the name of Jesus.

Righteous Father, whatever you are showing me that I am unwilling to delve into because I am feeling that it is not profitable, supply me with the grace to do what you have shown me in the name of Jesus.

Holy Father, I pray that you will supply me with the grace to abound in any place that you have shown me until that place begins to yield results in the name of Jesus.

Heavenly Father, by the reason of your shepherd role upon my life, financial abundance shall become my portion in the name of Jesus.

Gracious Father, I reject every spirit of poverty, lack, and want in my life in the name of Jesus.

Thank you Holy Father for hearing and answering my prayers because want and need have been terminated over my life in the name of Jesus.

CHAPTER 3

The Pastures

Psalm 23:2

> *He maketh me to lie down in green pastures*

Whenever the word green pasture is mentioned, the picture often painted in our minds is that of the green vegetation where everywhere is lush and luxuriant. With the sheep enjoying the coolness of the pasture after they have fed to their satisfaction. While this is the common picture that comes to mind, the revelation portrayed in the Scripture is not so.

It signifies a situation where we have gotten to in our walk with the Lord that we are living in abundance and satisfied in what the shepherd has done for us. This is not a place where we get to in a day. It is a place where God works on us before we get there. It could be that there are trials on the way, difficulty or even situations that make it seem as if God is not with us.

As a believer, you should never be discouraged by what you are currently going through. No matter how difficult it gets, it is the shepherd that is leading you to a place where the pasture is always green. Now, this is not a place where you will just come and go. Just as some believers experience some seasons of financial abundance, and everything disappears. The place where the shepherd is leading you to is a place of a permanent dwelling. Look at what the Bible says, that he makes me lie down in green pastures. The Bible did not say, he makes me visit green pastures. But that the Scripture says, he makes me lie down in green pastures indicating that what God is doing is permanent.

This is not something that happens in one day. It takes time and process for God to make you lie down in green pastures. The challenge is many of us are discouraged before we get to our permanent green pastures. God will have to work on your life so that when he puts you in the green pastures, you do not take your eyes off him and begin to focus it on the pasture that you are enjoying. Which is why before God blesses, he breaks.

Luke 22:19

> *And he took bread, and gave thanks, and brake it, and gave unto them, saying, This is my body which is given for you: this do in remembrance of me.*

When Jesus was given the bread, he gave thanks and broke it before giving it to the disciples. Before the bread could be given to the disciples so that it could bless the multitudes and satisfy their needs, it was broken. This is the normal progression of entering into the green pastures of life.

If God has not broken us before we enter into the green pastures, our affection will turn to the pasture rather than to him that has taken us into the green pasture. That is the problem that many believers are having that made it impossible for them to enter into the green pastures that the shepherd is taking them to.

God knows that there are a lot of things that have not been worked on. He sees a lot of greed. He sees a lot of selfishness. He sees a lot of withholding of resources after financial blessings have been poured on our lives. So God says before I will take you into the green pasture, let me do a little work on your life. So that in the place of the abundance of that green pasture, you will be able to take that which God has given you and bless others. You won't become a reservoir alone. But you will become a fountain of blessing that can give out the resources that God has entrusted into your hands.

The truth is that not all that God has given you is for your consumption. But if we have not been broken, that is the mentality that we will have. It is just about me, myself, and I. What others are going through even though we are living in financial abundance or the blessings of the Lord, won't bother us.

God will never allow us to enter into that green pasture if we have issues that need his spiritual attention.

So the prayer here is not just to enter into the green pastures that the shepherd wants to take you to. But to reveal what can hinder you from living in that green pasture. God working on us so that we can enter into that green pasture is more important than the green pasture itself. God does not want us to experience temporary green pastures. He wants us to lie down there and remain in that place for the remainder of our life on earth. I pray that God will help us to enter into the green pastures and remain there in the name of Jesus.

Scripture for Meditation

Revelation 7:17

> *For the Lamb which is in the midst of the throne shall feed them, and shall lead them unto living fountains of waters: and God shall wipe away all tears from their eyes.*

Prayer

Reflection

Ezekiel 34:14

> *I will feed them in a good pasture, and upon the high mountains of Israel shall their fold be: there shall they lie in a good fold, and in a fat pasture shall they feed upon the mountains of Israel.*

Isaiah 30:23

> *Then shall he give the rain of thy seed, that thou shalt sow the ground withal; and bread of the increase of the earth, and it shall be fat and plenteous: in that day shall thy cattle feed in large pastures.*

Thank you Righteous Father for the assurance which I have in your word that you will make me lie down in green pastures to you be all the glory and the honour in the name of Jesus.

Holy Father, whatever that is in my life that will stop me from entering into permanent green pastures, let it be removed in the name of Jesus.

Heavenly Father, where my entry into the green pastures has been delayed as a result of things that you needed to work on in my life, I ask that you do a quick work of righteousness so that I can enter into that green pasture and lie down there in the name of Jesus.

Gracious Father, where I have been struggling with the work you are doing in my life give me the grace to submit myself to the work that you have been doing there in the name of Jesus.

Righteous Father, I ask that you release upon me the patience that I need so that your work in my life can be completed for my entrance and lying down in the green pastures in the name of Jesus.

Holy Father, where I have been discouraged thinking that things haven't been working without knowing that you have been doing great work in my life so that I can enter and lie down in permanent green pastures, I ask that you forgive me and help me to overcome the spirit of discouragement in the name of Jesus.

Heavenly Father, help me to be broken in every area of my life so that I can lie down in that green pasture in the name of Jesus.

Righteous Father, where I have the tendency to take my eyes off you and put it in the pasture that is around my life, deliver me from that in the name of Jesus.

Holy Father, I know that everything you do takes time and process, help me to cooperate with you until the process is complete in the name of Jesus.

Gracious Father, help me to use this green pastures which you have made me lie down in to bless the lives of others around me in the name of Jesus.

Thank you for hearing and answering me in the name of Jesus.

CHAPTER 4

Still Waters

Psalm 23:2

> *he leadeth me beside the still waters.*

Every leading of God is distinguished by one critical factor – the still waters. And whenever the water is not still but turbulent and boisterous, it is an indication that the leading is not of God. The leading of God is always marked by the still waters. The still waters is an indication to you that the path you are taking is of God. When you look at the logos of the Scripture, the first question that may arise in your mind is the still waters means absence of trouble. If it is so, then the believer will never be faced with the bad situation of life. Everything will be good.

There is nowhere in the Scripture where it says God will lead us to goodly places all the time. Jesus was led by God into the wilderness to be tempted for 40 days. The wilderness is a dry place that supports very little living things. If God will lead his Son to the wilderness, then we the children of God cannot be exempted from being led to something that looks troublesome. And when God is leading you to a troublesome place, is because he has given you the capacity to overcome it. Jesus was led by the spirit of God into the wilderness to be tempted by the devil because God is fully aware that Jesus could overcome any temptation that the devil might throw at him.

When the Bible says he leads me beside the still waters, what the Scripture indicates is the presence of peace. Which is why the Bible says the water is still. If all of us as children of God can learn to trust in the still waters of his leading, we will never walk in trial and error. And the peace that God gives cannot be sustained by any factor. It is not the peace that money gives. Neither is it a peace that is brought about by a happy event or circumstances. It is a type of peace as the Bible states that the world cannot give.

John 14:27

> *Peace I leave with you, my peace I give unto you: not as the world giveth, give I unto you. Let not your heart be troubled, neither let it be afraid.*

Friends, this is where the errors of many believers lie. Some have disregarded the peace that the Lord gives and are living in regret today. Others have disregarded that peace at the detriment of the success of their business. No wonder the Bible says, I will listen to what the Lord will say because the Lord will speak peace. The earlier you learn this fact of the still waters, the better for you as a child of God. While the devil can contaminate other speaking of God, the devil can never fake the peace of God. You see, the Bible says it is the peace that the world cannot give. And who is the prince of the world? Jesus gives us an answer in the book of John 14:30

> *Hereafter I will not talk much with you: for the prince of this world cometh, and hath nothing in me.*

He said the Prince of this world came and found nothing in me. He was speaking of the devil.

Whatever that you want to go into as a believer, one of the strongest things you can rely on that God is involved in what you are doing is peace.

When peace is absent, God is not in it. Where peace is present, God is in it. It is that simple. Whenever you hear people say, I don't have peace over this matter, yet they are going in that direction which is against their peace, it is a signature for disaster. Some believers have embarked on journeys that they do not have peace, and they died in the process. Others entered into businesses that they do not have peace, and they lose thousands or millions of dollars. Some were married against their peace, and they are biting their fingers in regrets today. The still waters of God are something that the child of God should never take for granted. Which is why the Bible tells us in the book of Psalms, that God will lead us beside the still waters. And that still waters is the presence of the peace of God.

While other means of direction of God may take time to be able to comprehend them, peace is one of the easiest that even a baby believer can rely on. Once the believer knows that when he feels peace it is God, when he does not feel the peace it is not God, he can follow that leading. In the state of that immaturity, the believer can successfully follow the leading of God based on the peace that he feels.

And that peace is individualistic. It is not something that someone should feel for you because God has a personal relationship with each of his children. If God wants to show you that what you are doing he is not in it, there won't be peace. Never disregard your peace for the peace of another. Never throw away your peace based on what another person feels. Peace is personal to you alone. The story of the young prophet and the old prophet is what I will use in showing us that you shouldn't disregard your peace for that of another.

1 Kings 13:14-19

> *And went after the man of God,*
> *and found him sitting under an*
> *oak: and he said unto him, Art*

thou the man of God that camest from Judah? And he said, I am.

15 Then he said unto him, Come home with me, and eat bread.

16 And he said, I may not return with thee, nor go in with thee: neither will I eat bread nor drink water with thee in this place:

17 For it was said to me by the word of the Lord, Thou shalt eat no bread nor drink water there, nor turn again to go by the way that thou camest.

18 He said unto him, I am a prophet also as thou art; and an angel spake unto me by the word of the Lord, saying, Bring him back with thee into thine house, that he may eat bread and drink water. But he lied unto him.

19 So he went back with him, and did eat bread in his house, and drank water.

God told this young prophet to prophesy in the city and to ensure that he does not eat any food there. Another person came and told him who is much older, that he should eat food. Maybe this young prophet had a lot of peace when God was giving him the instruction of what he's supposed to do. Yet he threw away his conviction and that peace, for the peace of another older prophet. The result of the disobedience to the instruction of God led to his untimely demise.

1 Kings 13:23-25

And it came to pass, after he had eaten bread, and after he had drunk, that he saddled for him the ass, to wit, for the prophet whom he had brought back.

24 And when he was gone, a lion met him by the way, and slew him: and his carcase was cast in the way, and the ass stood by it, the lion also stood by the carcase.

25 And, behold, men passed by, and saw the carcase cast in the way, and the lion standing by the carcase: and they came and told it in the city where the old prophet dwelt.

Friends, the peace that we feel in our spirit is a signal to us that something isn't right. It is just like the conventional traffic light where red indicates danger, yellow indicates get ready. While green shows that you can go. That peace is not something we should joke with as children of God. God will always grant us his peace to show that he is either present or absent in what we are about to do. If we ignore it, we can walk into trouble. If we follow it, we can be saved from trouble. I pray that God will help us to follow the leading of his peace in the name of Jesus.

Scripture for Meditation

Ezekiel 34:15

> *I will feed my flock, and I will cause them to lie down, saith the Lord God.*

Prayers

Reflection

Isaiah 26:3

> *Thou wilt keep him in perfect peace, whose mind is stayed on thee: because he trusteth in thee.*

Leviticus 26:6

And I will give peace in the land,
and ye shall lie down, and none
shall make you afraid: and I will
rid evil beasts out of the land,
neither shall the sword go
through your land.

Thank you Holy Father for the assurance of your leading which is always beside the still waters. To you be all the glory and the honour in the name of Jesus.

Holy Father, I want to ask for mercy for every time that you have shown me your peace and I have disregarded it. I ask you to forgive me in the name of Jesus.

Heavenly Father, any time you place your peace in my heart to approve or disapprove of the step that I am about to take, release upon me the grace to follow that peace in the name of Jesus.

Gracious Father, although I hear your voice, hear you through dreams and other means of your communication, help me to master the art of the peace that you will lead me by in the name of Jesus.

Holy Father, you have said in your word that you will lead me beside the still waters. Let the reality of the Scripture be immediately activated in my life in the name of Jesus.

Gracious Father, whenever that I have fallen prey to the peace that the world gives, I ask you for mercy in the name of Jesus.

Heavenly Father, you have said in your word that we should be anxious for nothing but in everything let us do it by prayers and supplication and the peace of God will mount guard in my heart. I pray that that peace will forever be present whenever I seek your face for direction in the name of Jesus.

Thank you Holy Father for your peace by which I will be guided from now henceforth in the name of Jesus.

CHAPTER 5

Soul Restoration

Psalm 23:3

He restoreth my soul

King David was writing the Psalms from the perspective of the shepherd boy who was shouldering the responsibility of taking care of the sheep. He has seen that sometimes when he takes the sheep out to graze upon pastures, some of the sheep may be wounded. Others may have one form of affliction or the other. So whenever he brought the sheep back to the place where they are supposed to rest for the night, he will begin to check through the sheep to see those who require restoration.

In simple terms, to restore is to bring something back to the position where it was before the happening of a certain event. If a car had an accident, and it is to be restored, the restoration will bring it back to the place where it was before the accident. Although this is an example that relates to a car, it is pretty much the same thing that the shepherd does to the sheep. Those who require treatment will be treated by the shepherd, at least before they go out the next day. The shepherd is aware that without the restoration of the sheep to the state where they were, it will be impossible for them to go and graze when they are taken out next time.

The Lord as our shepherd performs the same responsibility of restoring our souls to the place where he wants it to be. Whenever we are injured as a result of what we are doing on the earth, the Lord restores our souls. Without restoration, that injury can remain and make lasting damage to our souls. This is a specialty of the shepherd, and he knows what best to do to be able to restore any believer.

The Lord restores the soul of the believer to enjoy the fullness of God. Not only the soul, but the Lord also restores everything that concerns us. It could be finances, health, relationship, etc., just to bring things to the way that they were before the happening of certain occurrences. The need for the restoration can be as a result of a betrayer, a difficulty which we have experienced, a loss of a loved one, or even an affliction of the body that distorts our perspective of who God is to us. Just as the shepherd restores the sheep, that is what the Lord does to us. He restores our souls so that we can continue to serve him and do his will.

How the restoration of the soul takes place may be different depending on the sheep involved.

No single sheep is practically the same as another. That is how every believer is different from another to reflect the uniqueness of God.

A classic example of the restoration of the soul took place in the life of Job. From the beginning of the book of Job, we saw that Job was one of the richest men of the East.

Job 1:1-3

> *There was a man in the land of Uz, whose name was Job; and that man was perfect and upright, and one that feared God, and eschewed evil.*
> *2 And there were born unto him seven sons and three daughters.*
> *3 His substance also was seven thousand sheep, and three thousand camels, and five hundred yoke of oxen, and five hundred she asses, and a very great household; so that this*

man was the greatest of all the
men of the east.

When God boasted about the faithfulness of Job, the enemy was allowed to test him. And when that test occurred, Job lost everything that he had. In the early chapter of the book of Job, the Bible tells us that he had 7000 sheep, 3000 camels, 500 yokes of oxen, 500 she-asses and a very great household. When the devil threw all his attacks against the life of Job, everything he had including his household was destroyed. But that was not the end of the story. God performs an excellent restoration in the life of Job. This restoration occurred in the book of Job 42:12-13:

So the Lord blessed the latter
end of Job more than his
beginning: for he had fourteen
thousand sheep, and six
thousand camels, and a
thousand yoke of oxen, and a
thousand she asses.

*13 He had also seven sons and
three daughters.*

After the restoration, the Bible tells us he has
14,000 sheep, 6000 camels, 8000 yokes of oxen,
and 1000 she asses. He also had seven sons and
three daughters. Not only did God restore what
Job had loss, but the restoration also doubled
everything that he possessed. In case you are
reading this book right now with a lot of
despair, I want to let you know that God is going
to restore your soul. He is a master in
restoration. Whatever it is that you have gone
through, whether it is ill-health, a severe attack
of the enemy that tested the faithfulness of God
in your life, backbiting and stabbing by the
brethren, rejection by family members, and all
types of affliction that can affect the child of
God on the earth, the Lord is going to restore
you just as he did to the life of Job.

Another perspective of the restoration of the
soul is the bringing back of the sheep that have
gone out of the sheepfold. When we are

referring to this type of sheep, I mean believers who were backslidden from the faith and returned to the life of sin. The Lord restores their soul to the place where it was before the backsliding. They will be back to serving the Lord as their Saviour. I have seen several people whom the Lord has been able to restore after going out of the sheepfold into the world. I pray that that great shepherd of the sheep will cause a restoration to happen in every area of your life in the name of Jesus.

Scripture for Meditation

Psalm 19:7

> *The law of the Lord is perfect, converting the soul: the testimony of the Lord is sure, making wise the simple.*

Reflection

Job 33:30

> *To bring back his soul from the pit, to be enlightened with the light of the living.*

Psalm 119:176

> *I have gone astray like a lost sheep; seek thy servant; for I do not forget thy commandments.*

Thank you Holy Father for the restoration of my soul which you are about to do I give you glory and honour in the name of Jesus.

Heavenly Father, I ask that you cause a complete restoration of my soul in the name of Jesus.

Holy Father, just as you restore the sheep to the state where they ought to be, that is how you will restore my finances to the place where it was in the name of Jesus.

Heavenly Father, I have seen in your word in the book of Job how that you restore him to the place where he was before the attack of the enemy. Restore my life today in the name of Jesus.

Holy Father, I know that as a shepherd, part of what you do is the restoration of the sheep. I pray that you cause a restoration of my health to the place where it was before this affliction in the name of Jesus.

Gracious Father, anything that I have gone through in life which has distorted my perspective of who you are as a faithful God, I ask that you restore me in the name of Jesus.

Gracious Father, let your healing balm heal my emotions and cause a restoration there in the name of Jesus.

Holy Father, I pray for (mention the name of the person who has veered off from the faith if you know) that you restore this person into the sheepfold in the name of Jesus.

Holy Father, just as you restored the life of Job to have double of what he possessed before the attack of the enemy, do that same restoration for my life in the name of Jesus.

Thank you, father, for hearing and answering my prayers to you be all the glory and honour in the name of Jesus.

CHAPTER 6

His Leading

Psalm 23:3

> he leadeth me in the paths of
> righteousness for his name's
> sake.

Every leading of God must be subject to this ultimate test – he leads me in the path of righteousness. If whatever that God is leading you to is not in the path of righteousness that can never be God. All the leading of God must be in the path of righteousness. This is one of the ways to distinguish between the leading of the devil and the leading of God. While God will lead you in the path of righteousness, the devil will lead you in the path of evil. After all, he's single and ultimate goal is to kill, steal, and destroy. That is his mission statement.

And one way to be able to checkmate the deception of Satan in leading is to stick to the word of God. It is the entire word of God that defines to you what is righteousness. It will not be the leading of God that will tell you to go and take your neighbour's wife. It will also not be the leading of God that will tell you to take what does not belong to you. It will not be the leading of God that will tell you to fornicate. All of these out rightly go against scriptural truth. If anyone has been led in this path, it is not the leading of God. If the shepherd is the one leading you, it must be in the path of righteousness and no more. Anything other than this is not the shepherd, but the wolf that came to scatter the sheep. Or even a beer or a lion whose intent is to destroy the sheep and scatter them. Just as David explained to King Saul when he came before him at the battleground that a lion and a bear came to kill the sheep (2 Samuel 17:34-35).

The personality by which the leading of God in the path of righteousness is expressed in the life of every believer is the Holy Spirit. Any leading that God will give any believer in our present dispensation will be by the Holy Spirit. The Bible speaking concerning the ministry of the Holy Spirit in the life of believers says in the book of John 16:13:

> *Howbeit when he, the Spirit of truth, is come, he will guide you into all truth: for he shall not speak of himself; but whatsoever he shall hear, that shall he speak: and he will shew you things to come.*

It is the responsibility of the Holy Spirit to lead us into all truth. This is in line with what is contained in the Bible in the book of Psalms 23:3. This is not a Scripture that we pray into our lives alone. There is a portion of it that requires our obedience. In essence, even if you pray that God should lead you in the path of righteousness for the sake of his name, he will do so. After all, God is faithful to all that he has said out of his mouth. The challenge is when he wants to lead us, are we going to follow his leading?

The Holy Spirit is ever willing to lead any believer in the path of righteousness who has a sincere heart. No matter how the Holy Spirit desires to lead you if you have idols in your heart, it will hinder that leading.

Ezekiel 14:3

> *Son of man, these men have set up their idols in their heart, and put the stumblingblock of their iniquity before their face:*

should I be inquired of at all by them?

What are those idols? I will give you an example. A believer may be asking God for the choice of which university he should go to. Yet at the corner of his mind, he has already made his choice. Or a sister may be praying to God to choose which of the various men that proposed to her should be her husband. However, among the three people that came, she has already made up her mind on one of them. That is an idol and it can hinder the leading of the Holy Spirit in the path of righteousness.

Before you come to God to ask for anything, let your heart be empty. If you have already decided, what is the purpose of seeking to be led? The Holy Spirit will always be there to guide you as a believer if only you will be sincere to him. And all his leading will be in the path of righteousness.

For us not to glory in our achievements, the Bible tells us in the book of Psalms 23:3 that God will lead us in the path of righteousness for his name's sake. Have you been led and the leading of the Holy Spirit produced a financial breakthrough? Have you been led in your life to marry a man or woman and that marriage has been a blessing to all the people around your life? Have you been led to study a course at the university and that has produced outstanding results? Have you been led to start a business and that business has turned around your financial fortune? I want you to remember something, that God did it for the sake of his name. It is not because you are exceptional, intelligent, well-trained, the best or any other physical qualification that you can think of. It is for the sake of his name only.

I pray that God will keep us humble while he leads us in the path of righteousness in the name of Jesus.

Scripture for Meditation

Psalm 25:5

> *Lead me in thy truth, and teach me: for thou art the God of my salvation; on thee do I wait all the day.*

Reflection

Psalm 5:8

> *Lead me, O Lord, in thy righteousness because of mine enemies; make thy way straight before my face.*

Psalm 85:13

> *Righteousness shall go before him; and shall set us in the way of his steps.*

Prayer

Thank you Holy Father for the leading that you have led me so far in my life to you be all the glory and the honour in the name of Jesus.

Holy Father, let the leading of the Holy Spirit be activated in every area of my life in the name of Jesus.

Heavenly Father, I know that even if the Holy Spirit is going to lead me in the path of righteousness for his namesake, I also need to obey the leading. I pray for the release of the grace to obey the leading of the Holy Spirit in the name of Jesus.

Gracious Father, baptise me with the willingness to obey the leading of the Holy Spirit in every area of my life in the name of Jesus.

Holy Father, you have said in your word that if I am willing and obedient, I will eat the good of the land. Let the Holy Spirit lead me to the good of the land in the path of righteousness in the name of Jesus.

Heavenly Father, help me to remain humble while the leading of the Holy Spirit produces exceptional results in my life in the name of Jesus.

Holy Father, whatever it is that can hinder the leading of the Holy Spirit in my life in the path of righteousness, let that thing be removed in the name of Jesus.

Gracious Father, every idol in my heart that can prevent the Holy Spirit from leading me, purge that idol from my heart in the name of Jesus.

Thank you Holy Father for hearing and answering all of my prayers and petition before your throne at this hour, to you be all the glory and the honour in the name of Jesus.

CHAPTER 7

Psalm 23:4

> *Yea, though I walk through the valley of the shadow of death, I will fear no evil: for thou art with me;*

The Shadow of Death

As believers who have been redeemed by the precious blood of the lamb, we are not afraid of death. The Bible tells us that, precious is the death of the saints in the sight of the Lord. Paul the apostle in one of his Epistles captures it succinctly as for me to live is Christ and to die is gain (Philippians 1:21). But a child of God can walk through the valley of the shadow of death in his life.

Some believers are currently walking through it, and some will walk through that valley. There are several situations of life that the believer can go through that is like the valley of the shadow of death. So many believers have been through that valley. It could be extreme lack, the sickness that is threatening to shut the breath of God in our nostrils, and various situations that we have prayed and prayed and nothing seems to change. Listen to what the Bible says, I shall not be afraid. He has already promised and will never renege on his words that he will never leave us nor forsake us. If you are going through the darkest moment of your life now, don't let fear plant his feet on your life.

Whenever we walk through the valley of the shadow of death, the devil will come with his suggestions, lies, and deceits. He will be speaking these words constantly into our ears. Are you sure that God hasn't forgotten about you? If God is indeed faithful, why hasn't he healed you? Why did he let Eric die? Why did my mom have to suffer? Why, why, and why. These are the prominent questions that preoccupy a believer in the valley of the shadow of death.

2 Corinthians 4:17

> *For our light affliction, which is but for a moment, worketh for us a far more exceeding and eternal weight of glory;*

So even the valley of the shadow of death is for a moment. Armed yourself with the thought that no matter how tough it gets, it will end one day.

What do you do when you are at the valley of the shadow of death?

1. There must be light at the end of the tunnel (valley). I want you to realise that there is light at the end of the tunnel. When you pass through that valley, be fully aware that there is light at the end of the valley. No matter how difficult the situation gets, one day it will come to an end. The Bible said though I walk through the valley of the shadow of death. You are supposed to pass through it and not live in it. So ensure you come out of it. Don't die there. God may allow you to pass to the valley, but he doesn't want you to make a tent there. I pray that God will supply you with the grace to come out of the valley in the name of Jesus.

2. Remember the stories of others. Are there people around your life who have been through the most difficult moments of life similar to the one that you are going through? And you saw that those people came out of the valley. If there are, that is to serve as an encouragement to you that

you will also come out of it. If there are no people around you to serve as an encouragement, remember the stories of others in the Bible. For example, the story of Job. After passing through the valley, God brought him out of it successfully. If God can do it for Job, he will do it for you too.

3. There is a double promotion. After every valley of the shadow of death, comes double promotion. Whatever it is that you are going through after that valley, you are coming out with God's promotion. Look at the life of Job for example after what he went through and his experience in the valley he was given double of all that he had before that encounter with the valley.

4. Never fear. The fear that I am alone will always be felt in the valley. Is the Lord with me or has he left me? We all ask the same question. When the Israelites were confronted with tough situations in the

wilderness, they asked, is the Lord among us or not? (Exodus 17:7). Refuse to allow fear to take a grip of your life. When Satan comes with all his suggestions of fear, reject them. Don't allow yourself to fall into his trap of despair. May the Lord help us all in the name of Jesus.

Scripture for Meditation

Isaiah 43:2

> *When thou passest through the waters, I will be with thee; and through the rivers, they shall not overflow thee: when thou walkest through the fire, thou shalt not be burned; neither shall the flame kindle upon thee.*

Reflection

Psalm 3:6

I will not be afraid of ten thousands of people, that have set themselves against me round about.

Psalm 27:1

The Lord is my light and my salvation; whom shall I fear? the Lord is the strength of my life; of whom shall I be afraid?

Prayers

Thank You Holy Father for the grace that I have been enjoying even though I am in the valley of the shadow of death. To you be all the glory in the name of Jesus.

Holy Father, I ask for mercy where I have allowed my entire focus to be consumed by the valley of the shadow of death in the name of Jesus.

Heavenly Father, where I have allowed the lies of the enemy to fill my ears, I asked for mercy in the name of Jesus.

Holy Father, I ask that you supply me with the grace to come out of this valley of the shadow of death stronger than I was in the name of Jesus.

Gracious Father, I pray that you will pour an overwhelming promotion over my life after this valley is over in the name of Jesus.

Holy Father, I pray that you will supply me with the grace and strength to focus my eyes on the glory at the end of the valley in the name of Jesus.

Heavenly Father, I reject every spirit of fear that the enemy has released upon my life during this valley in the name of Jesus.

Gracious Father I declare today that this valley shall not swallow me, but I am walking through the valley and coming out of it in the name of Jesus.

Holy Father, I reject every spirit of discouragement that the devil has fired into my life as a result of this valley in the name of Jesus.

Righteous Father, just as you brought Job out of the valley, so will you bring me out of the valley in the name of Jesus.

Holy Father, I ask that you will help me to understand that no valley will last forever in the name of Jesus.

CHAPTER 8

Psalm 23:4

for thou art with me;

You are with me

It is not all the time that you feel the presence of the shepherd with his staff standing over you. Often, we feel nothing. And feelings sometimes are the agents of deception. If we continue to walk by what we feel, we will think that the shepherd isn't with us. The thing isn't my

71

feeling but by faith. The shepherd has already promised that he would never leave us nor forsake us. Sometimes when things befall us, the impression created by circumstances is that the shepherd has left us alone to face the situation that is now threatening us. The Scriptures tells us that the angels of the Lord are around those who fear him and they deliver them (Psalm 34:7)

Friends, have anything presented a contrary picture to you that God isn't with you? Even in the face of that picture, know that the Lord is with you. It is the presence of the shepherd with you that determines what you can stand when trouble comes your way. When presenting his account to Saul for what he did for the sheep, David told him that he killed a bear and the lion. If David wasn't with the sheep, the lion and the bear would have scattered them and destroyed anyone that they chose. The presence of the shepherd with the sheep determines what they can stand and who can attack them. Whenever the shepherd is absent, the sheep are vulnerable to all sorts of attack. Which is the reason why the shepherd is always with the sheep. I will show you an example in the Scriptures how the presence of the shepherd determines what the sheep can withstand.

Mark 4:36-39

36 And when they had sent away the multitude, they took him even as he was in the ship. And there were also with him other little ships.

37 And there arose a great storm of wind, and the waves beat into the ship, so that it was now full.

38 And he was in the hinder part of the ship, asleep on a pillow: and they awake him, and say unto him, Master, carest thou not that we perish?

> *39 And he arose, and rebuked the wind, and said unto the sea, Peace, be still. And the wind ceased, and there was a great calm.*

The disciples of Jesus Christ were in the boat while Jesus was sleeping. The wind became so tempestuous that it threatened to destroy the boat and all the people in it. Something very strange was happening when the wind was tossing the boat on the surface of the water. Jesus was sleeping and was never disturbed by the strong wind. While the wind was troubling, Jesus knew that nothing was going to happen as long as he's in the boat with them. Here, we see that the presence of the shepherd was the only factor responsible for the preservation of the life of the disciples. Since the shepherd was with the disciples, their lives must be preserved. Do you see the reason why the Bible says in the book of Psalms 23:4 that thou art with me!

Moses was another man who understood the value of the presence of the shepherd. When they were about to travel into the wilderness to confront some nations in the way, Moses insisted that unless the Lord goes with them, he won't move an inch.

Exodus 33:15

> *And he said unto him, If thy presence go not with me, carry us not up hence.*

Even when the Lord assured Moses that he was going to send an angel, Moses did not change his request. If you won't go with us, we will go nowhere. He continued his importunate demand until the Lord granted him his request. I will go with you.

Exodus 33:17

> *And the Lord said unto Moses, I will do this thing also that thou hast spoken: for thou hast*

found grace in my sight, and I
know thee by name.

Moses knows that if the shepherd was with them, no nation will have the power to withstand them or resist their journey. And we all know the story of the children of the Israelites how they went through the desert and conquered all the nations that were about them. What gave them the temerity in the desert is the presence of the shepherd. If the shepherd is with you, there is nothing that you cannot conquer and there is nothing that can conquer you. No matter how the battle rages, you are going to come out strong as a winner and not as a loser.

Sometimes it is possible to begin to ask a lot of serious question and doubt the presence of the shepherd around your life especially when the believer is passing through a difficult situation. The truth is that the shepherd has already promised to be with you and he won't let you go alone. If David as a shepherd boy did not run away from the sheep in the face of the threat to his life posed by the lion and the bear, what made you feel that God who is our shepherd would leave us at a time when we needed him the most? The truth is that it is not by your feelings that the Lord is with you. Neither is it the defining circumstances that tell you whether God is with you or not. It is by the promise of God in the Scripture that tells us that he's with us all the time. When Jesus was about to send the disciples to go and preach in the whole nations of the earth he gave them an important promise: *"lo I am with you till the end of the age"* (Matthew 28:18)

The presence of the shepherd is the only anchor for your soul. It will hold you if only you can have the consciousness that he is with you. When we forget that the presence of the shepherd is with us, we begin to doubt and listen to the devil more. And the devil being the liar that he is will continue to fill our hearts and ears with lies that God has forgotten us.

Friends, you have been asking questions that God is not with you. But I also want to ask you a question, and I wished you will be sincere to answer it. Do you know the reason why things haven't got bad? It is because the shepherd is with you. If the shepherd wasn't with you, that sickness that you went through would have killed you. If the shepherd wasn't with you, that debt you had would have put you in serious trouble. If the shepherd wasn't with you, that terrible accident you had would have killed you. All that you have been through the presence of the shepherd was the reason why what you experienced didn't grow worse. I pray that the Lord will help us in the name of Jesus to know that the shepherd is always with us.

Scripture for Meditation

Psalm 37:25

I have been young, and now am old; yet have I not seen the righteous forsaken, nor his seed begging bread.

Reflection

Hebrews 13:5

Let your conversation be without covetousness; and be content with such things as ye have: for he hath said, I will never leave thee, nor forsake thee.

Genesis 28:15

And, behold, I am with thee, and will keep thee in all places whither thou goest, and will bring thee again into this land; for I will not leave thee, until I have done that which I have spoken to thee of.

Prayers

Thank You Holy Father for your everlasting presence that has never left me for a single day. To you be all the glory and the honour in the name of Jesus.

Heavenly Father, I want to ask you for mercy in any situation that I have doubted the presence of the shepherd with me. Any time that I have believed in the situation more than in the capacity of the shepherd to help me, I ask that you show me mercy and forgiveness in the name of Jesus.

Holy Father, I ask that you baptise me with the consciousness of the shepherd being with me all the time in the name of Jesus.

Gracious Father, I pray that because of the presence of the shepherd with me this mountain that I have been going through, will never swallow me in the name of Jesus.

Righteous Father, as long as you are with me, no situation of life can overpower me in the name of Jesus.

Gracious Father, grant me the grace to put my faith in the ability of the shepherd to keep me and help me all the time in the name of Jesus.

Holy Father, just as your presence prevented the boat of the disciples from capsizing that is how your presence will prevent this ill-health from overpowering me in the name of Jesus.

Gracious Father, may the presence of the shepherd give me the grace to withstand every tough situation of life in the name of Jesus.

Thank you mighty Father for hearing and answering my prayers, to you be all the glory and the honour in the name of Jesus.

CHAPTER 9

Psalm 23:4

> *thy rod and thy staff they comfort me.*

The Rod and the Staff

The rod and the staff represent the two-dimensional aspect of the shepherd. He has a rod for discipline and also staff for guidance. No shepherd can function effectively without the two.

The Rod

The Bible in the book of Proverbs aptly gives us a directive lesson that if we spare the rod, we hate the child.

Proverbs 13:24

> *He that spareth his rod hateth his son: but he that loveth him chasteneth him betimes.*

And this is true for every shepherd. There are times that restive sheep may need the use of the rod to correct them or restore them to perfect alignment or where the shepherd wants them to be. The purpose of the rod is not to destroy the sheep but to express the love of the shepherd through discipline.

Even though the shepherd loves the sheep and could put his life on the stake for them, it won't bar him from using the rod where need be. David was inspired by the Holy Spirit to scribe these words to capture the relationship between the shepherd and the sheep. When the shepherd applies the rod, the sheep would probably be confused why would the same shepherd who put his life in danger before the bear or the lion be using the rod on them. But without the rod, the sheep would take for granted the expressive love of the shepherd. And this is what the shepherd does to keep the sheep in perfect order so that they will be where the shepherd wants them to be.

Every child of God experiences this loving disciplinary dimension of the shepherd, our Lord. And the purpose of our discipline when we have erred is for the destruction of our flesh and the salvation of our souls. Paul the apostle captures the essence of the rod of the shepherd in the book of Hebrews 12:11:

> *Now no chastening for the present seemeth to be joyous, but grievous: nevertheless afterward it yieldeth the peaceable fruit of righteousness*

> *unto them which are exercised*
> *thereby.*

The shepherd knows that without the chastisement and application of the rod when necessary, the sheep would be bastards as if they do not have a shepherd over them. And God does not want bastard children. Hebrews 12:5-8:

> *But if ye be without*
> *chastisement, whereof all are*
> *partakers, then are ye bastards,*
> *and not sons.*

As a nation, America is where it is today because the rod has been spared. Laws have been enacted against the discipline of our children, and because we have rejected the divine injunction restiveness among our children has sprung up in every nook and cranny of our land. Now, don't tell me that God put these words in the Scripture for fanciful decorations. I believe that they are meant to be obeyed. The application of this scriptural injunction is very weighty. If we want our children to be who God wants them, we need to apply that biblical directive.

Now don't get me wrong, I don't want anybody to misquote me. I do not support that anyone should beat his child carelessly. Any discipline that is out of order, is not of God. So what I'm talking about here is not excessive discipline.

If God chastises us, the purpose is entirely for good. I remember when I was young before my father went to be with the Lord, he used to chastise and beat me when I go wrong. At that point, it sounded as if he hated me. But I can tell you that he didn't. It was all for my good. As I look decades back, I can say that if Papa hadn't done what he did, you might not be reading this book that you are holding now. God used him mightily to put my excesses under constant check, and I am thankful to him. When my work is over, and I get to meet my earthly father in heaven, we will talk about some of these things.

The rod of the shepherd carries serious importance for our Christian walk. If the shepherd allows us, some of us would have veered off into the life of sin, in union with the former way of life that we once despised. Is God chastening you today? Don't despise it, it is for your good.

You won't tell me because your two-year-old does not want drugs, you won't administer it on him when you know that he has a fever. You will do so even if he doesn't want it. His hatred for drugs hasn't overridden its importance at that moment. You will insist that he takes the drugs because if he doesn't, that simple fever can kill him.

I remember one rainy Africa night when I was back in Africa. The rains were pummeling on the roof of the house, while thunder and lightning snapped several photographic shots of light upon the house that I was living. My aunty had to fix something in the rain, and a little boy was handed to me. He cried hard so that I would allow him to follow my aunty into the rain, but as hard as he increased the volume of his cry, I wasn't moved at all. I held him against my chest, and I wasn't bothered. As he continued his ear-piercing cries on that rainy night, the Holy Spirit intersperse with an important lesson to me.

"You wouldn't let this boy go into the rain because it is not good for him even though he is crying that he wants to. This is how God deals with his children too."

There can be no proper sons without discipline. The rod is always there to perform the necessary duty of keeping the sheep disciplined.

The Staff

While the rod performs the function of discipline, the staff does something different.

Romans 11:22

Behold therefore the goodness and severity of God: on them which fell, severity; but toward thee, goodness, if thou continue in his goodness: otherwise thou also shalt be cut off.

The Bible tells us that behold the goodness and the severity of God. There are always two sides to God. He is the lion and the lamb. He is the beginning and the end. He is the first and the last. The two aspects of God must be fully comprehended by the believer which is why there is both the rod and the staff. The staff reveals the caring dimension of the shepherd. He will go around them and use the staff to guide the sheep to where he wants them to go. And that is what the staff represents to us. The sad thing is that many of us know the staff of the shepherd without understanding the usefulness of the rod.

No discipline is ever complete without the use of the staff. Some of the so-called discipline that some of us do if weighed against this scripture would hardly stand. We disciplined and let the person go without using the staff to comfort the person. The staff is used to bring the person back after the use of the rod.

Both the staff and the rod are necessary for the sheep. May the Lord help us all to know the usefulness of both the staff and the rod in the name of Jesus.

Scripture for Meditation

Psalm 110:2

> *The Lord shall send the rod of thy strength out of Zion: rule thou in the midst of thine enemies.*

Reflection

Micah 7:14

*Feed thy people with thy rod,
the flock of thine heritage,
which dwell solitarily in the
wood, in the midst of Carmel:
let them feed in Bashan and
Gilead, as in the days of old.*

Psalms 73:14

*For all the day long have I been
plagued, and chastened every
morning.*

Prayer

Thank you Holy Father for your rod and staff
which you have made available for my discipline
and my care on the face of the earth to you be
all the glory and the honour in the name of
Jesus.

Holy Father, open my eyes to understand that
the purpose of the discipline upon my life is for
my spiritual growth in the name of Jesus.

Heavenly Father, forgive me for all the times I have taken for granted your chastisement upon my life in the name of Jesus.

Gracious Father, help me to be the sheep that the shepherd will guide so easily with his staff in the name of Jesus.

Holy Father, where rebellion has taken over my life, show me mercy and give me the grace to be the sheep that will always follow the guidelines of the shepherd in the name of Jesus.

Righteous Father, I pray that you will help me to understand that the reason why the shepherd is not sparing the rod is so that I would grow into the fullness of what God has ordained for me in the name of Jesus.

Thank you holy father for hearing and answering my prayers, in the name of Jesus.

CHAPTER 10

Psalm 23:5

> *Thou preparest a table before me in the presence of mine enemies:*

Preparing a Table

Towards the middle of the year 2019, I visited a sister in Christ that I have known for many years. Even though we were in the same city, Abuja, Nigeria, our work schedule never allowed us to meet. Then in the year 2019, we agreed to meet at her house. I drove from where

I was to meet her. I entered her home, and I was taken aback by the setting of a table. It was well prepared with all sort of cuisines to choose from. All manner of fruits incomprehensibly dotted the table. I sat on the table and feasted on all manner of fruits that satisfied me.

In the same way that the sister in Christ prepared this table for me to come and eat, and fellowship with her, that is the same way that the Lord prepares a table for us. The Lord will not only prepare a table for us, he does it amazingly. He prepares the table and set it amid our enemies. What a way that the shepherd uses to humiliate our enemies. They can't just do anything about it but watched as we lavishly feed on the table that the shepherd has prepared for us. That is the reason why sometimes when you pray for judgement to fall upon your enemies, the Lord may not answer all of the prayers. The reason is simple, if all the enemies are killed, before whom will the Lord set the table?

The table is not prepared before your friends or those who love you. The table is prepared in the presence of your enemies so that their anger and hatred can come out through their mouths. They hated you, but the Lord has prepared a financial table right before their eyes. Even amid hatred, you are succeeding financially. They hated you at your job, yet promotion kept coming because the Lord has prepared a table for you in their presence. They have no choice but to continue to watch you eat what the Lord has prepared for you.

How amazing it is to be a sheep of the shepherd. Your life will be subject to continuous feasting in the presence of your enemies. And this table that the Lord prepared for you is not only for eating alone. If you are barren and some people have mocked you, the Lord will also prepare a table for you that they will have to see you carry your baby before their eyes. If you have been mocked and put down that nothing good is going to come out of your life, the Lord will prepare a table for you in their presence, so that they can watch you as you feast in the blessings and the glory of God.

Friends, the Lord is going to prepare a table for you in the presence of your enemies. The only condition for you to feast on this table for the rest of your life is to be his sheep.

Scripture for Meditation

Psalm 22:26

> *The meek shall eat and be satisfied: they shall praise the Lord that seek him: your heart shall live for ever.*

Reflection

Psalm 31:19

> *Oh how great is thy goodness, which thou hast laid up for them that fear thee; which thou*

*hast wrought for them that
trust in thee before the sons of
men!*

Job 36:16

*Even so would he have removed
thee out of the strait into a
broad place, where there is no
straitness; and that which
should be set on thy table
should be full of fatness.*

Thank You Holy Father for the table that you
have set for me in the presence of my enemies
to you be all the glory and honour in the name
of Jesus.

Holy Father, I have seen in your word that you
prepare a table for me in the presence of my
enemies, I ask that let the Scripture become a
reality in my life in the name of Jesus.

Heavenly Father, I have understood by the
revelation that the table you prepare for me in

the presence of my enemies, is not just a table for eating alone. You can prepare for me a financial table, a success table, a blessing table, and a table of promotion so that I can feast in the presence of my enemies. I pray that you will prepare a table for me (mention the particular table that you want the Lord to prepare for you amid your enemies) so that I may feast to their shame and your glory in the name of Jesus.

Holy Father, help me to understand that in every situation of life that I go through, a time will come that you will prepare a table for me in the presence of my enemies in the name of Jesus.

Heavenly Father, let the manifestation of the Scripture in the book of Psalms 23, that you prepare a table for me in the presence of my enemies be manifested to everyone around me in the name of Jesus.

Holy Father, as I eat to my satisfaction from the table you have prepared for me in the presence of my enemies, let me be a blessing to others from that table in the name of Jesus.

Thank You Gracious Father for hearing and answering my prayers to you be all the glory and the honour in the name of Jesus.

CHAPTER 11

Psalm 23:5

thou anointest my head with oil

The oil

The shepherd anoints the head of the sheep with oil. There are several reasons why the shepherd does that. In certain seasons of the year, flies hover around the sheep so that they can lay eggs. If the head of the sheep is without oil, they lay their eggs on the sheep and this could result in the death of the sheep as they try to trash things around them to get rid of the flies. Without the oil on the head of the sheep, they are predisposed to a lot of deadly diseases and flies at particular seasons of the year. So the shepherd anoints ahead of the sheep to keep them protected from some of these flies and diseases while they graze around.

In the same way that the oil is a mark of preservation of the life of the sheep, that is the same way that the Lord as our shepherd anoints our ahead as a mark of preservation. When you have been anointed with oil, it is a mark of God's protection over your life. Which is why the Bible says touch, not my anointed and do my prophet no harm. If you are always touched and attacked by the enemy, both humans and spiritual agents of darkness that may be a sign that the anointing oil is lacking over your head because if the shepherd pours his oil on your head, you are untouchable.

God was using David to paint a graphic picture of what he does to all of his children who are his sheep. He anoints our head with oil to prevent every devil and human agent from bothering us. I'm going to give you some scriptural examples of how some who had the oil of the shepherd on their heads were preserved.

Abraham

Abraham was a man that had the anointing of the shepherd upon his life, and that anointing became the source of his preservation. Any time anybody tries to touch him, the anointing fought back. He was such an anointed man no one could dare touch him, and those who attempted almost paid the ultimate price of death.

Genesis 20:3

> But God came to Abimelech in a dream by night, and said to him, Behold, thou art but a dead man, for the woman which thou hast taken; for she is a man's wife.

Abimelech took Abraham's wife because of her extreme beauty. When God came to Abimelech, he told him you are a dead man. God did not tell Abimelech you will surely die. But you are already dead. You are already a dead man unless you restore unto Abraham his wife. What was fighting Abimelech? The oil of the shepherd upon the life of Abraham. As long as that oil was there, it will fight for him. Abraham did not even know that God was dealing with Abimelech. When they collected his wife, he just watched helplessly.

Friends, the anointing of the shepherd upon your life will do for you what you can never imagine. In most cases, the anointing will be working without you knowing it. It will be fighting battles that you never know, it will be dealing with the enemies that you have never seen and known. If there is anything that you need right now, is the anointing of the shepherd upon your life. The moment that anointing makes contact with your head, you become untouchable to principalities and powers and satanic human agents. Whenever your name is mentioned anywhere, they are aware that your life is out of bounds for them. So they advise other smaller demons and powers, if you do not want trouble, leave that brother or that sister alone. Don't you see the oil of the shepherd upon his head or are you so blind as not to see the oil of the shepherd upon the head?

Pharaoh also tried to take Sarah from the hands of Abraham.

Genesis 12:15-18

> *The princes also of Pharaoh saw her, and commended her before Pharaoh: and the woman was taken into Pharaoh's house.*
> *16 And he entreated Abram well for her sake: and he had sheep, and oxen, and he asses, and menservants, and*

maidservants, and she asses, and camels.

17 And the Lord plagued Pharaoh and his house with great plagues because of Sarai Abram's wife.

18 And Pharaoh called Abram, and said, What is this that thou hast done unto me? why didst thou not tell me that she was thy wife?

The moment he did that, the oil of the shepherd upon the life of Abraham began to fight back intensely. Pharaoh's entire household was plagued. When they knew that it was the wife of Abraham which they took that was behind their suffering, they told Abraham to take his wife and go his way. That is the power of the oil of the shepherd upon the life of a child of God. That oil will continue to be upon your life as long as you remain his sheep. Remember the shepherd anoints the head of the sheep every day for their preservation at some seasons of the year. If you stop being his sheep for a season, you will be vulnerable to attack of the enemy in that season. Do you see the reason why it is good to be the sheep of the shepherd all the time?

David

David was also a man that received the oil of the shepherd even though the Holy Spirit inspired him to write the Scripture in the book of Psalms 23. The Bible tells us in the book of 1 Samuel 16: 13:

> *Then Samuel took the horn of oil, and anointed him in the midst of his brethren: and the Spirit of the Lord came upon David from that day forward. So Samuel rose up, and went to Ramah.*

The moment the oil was poured upon the life of David, the anointing made him indestructible by the armoury of King Saul. Saul was envious of the fact that David would become King. So he made every determined effort to kill David. No matter how sustained his effort became, he couldn't kill him. Why? The anointing of the shepherd was upon the sheep, who is David. And as long as the anointing of the shepherd was upon his life, he could not be killed.

Jacob

After labouring for his uncle, Laban, Jacob made a decisive decision to return to his father's house. He told his two wives, Rachel and Leah, that he would be leaving the services of his cheating uncle, Laban. Unbeknown to Laban, Jacob left his house with his two wives and children. When Laban realised that Jacob left, he prepared to go and meet Jacob. In the night, the Lord appeared to Laban in the dream. The warning that came from that dream was stern.

Genesis 31:24:

> *And God came to Laban the Syrian in a dream by night, and said unto him, Take heed that thou speak not to Jacob either good or bad.*

Laban was warned and rebuked severely by God not to say anything to Jacob either good or bad. In other words, this Jacob you are about to talk to has the oil of the shepherd upon his head. If you talk to him carelessly, you will face me as his shepherd. And you know what, out of the fear of the shepherd Laban couldn't say anything to him either good or bad.

Friends, beyond the protective dimension of the anointing of the shepherd upon your life, the anointing can also help you to serve God. When the oil was poured upon the life of David, he later became King. No matter what you are doing, the oil of the shepherd needs to come upon your head. Are you in business? There is an oil that the shepherd will pour upon your head for succeeding in that business. Are you in ministry? There is also an oil that the shepherd will pour upon your head that will distinguish you in ministry and give you a voice to be heard in your generation. Are you a teacher or someone who is into education? There is an oil that the shepherd can pour upon your head that will make you one of the best sought after teachers in the whole of your country. Are you a politician or even an aspiring one? There is an anointing that the shepherd can pour upon your life that will make you be a politician with a big difference.

Friends, whatever you do in life there is an oil for succeeding in that thing. Even as a medical doctor, there is an oil that will make you succeed in your practice of medicine. What do you need to do? Get connected to the shepherd, his oil will rest on your head.

Scripture for Meditation

Psalms 92:10

> *But my horn shalt thou exalt like the horn of an unicorn: I shall be anointed with fresh oil.*

Reflection

2 Corinthians 1:21

> *Now he which stablisheth us with you in Christ, and hath anointed us, is God;*

Psalm 45:7

> *Thou lovest righteousness, and hatest wickedness: therefore God, thy God, hath anointed thee with the oil of gladness above thy fellows.*

Thank You Holy Father for the oil that you pour upon my head frequently as your sheep. I do not take this privilege for granted in the name of Jesus.

Holy Father, I want to thank you for the special privilege granted unto me to be your sheep. I know that there are many out there who are deserving of this opportunity more than me, but I know that it is the gift of God and not of strength so that no one can boast. Receive all the glory and the honour in the name of Jesus.

Holy Father, help me to carry the consciousness of the fact that the oil of the shepherd is always upon my life for my protection in the name of Jesus.

Heavenly Father, I pray that let the oil of the shepherd come upon my life for service in the ministry you have called me to in the name of Jesus.

Gracious Father, let the oil of the shepherd that is upon my head fight all of my battles in the name of Jesus.

Righteous Father, whatever it is that is contending with my peace as your sheep, let that thing or person receive the judgemental portion of the oil of the shepherd upon my life in the name of Jesus.

Holy Father, I pray that you will cause a divine visitation upon all those who are attacking my life just as the way you did to Abraham when Abimelech took his wife and also to Jacob when Laban wanted to talk to him. Cause divine visitation to happen to my enemies right now in the name of Jesus.

Thank You Holy Father for hearing and answering my prayers, I am grateful in the name of Jesus.

CHAPTER 12

Psalm 23:5

my cup runneth over.

My Cup

Shortly after the Lord has prepared a table for you in the presence of your enemies, the Bible tells us something very instructive. Your cup is going to run over. The Scripture flows from the feast which the Lord has prepared for us in the presence of our enemies. This is indicative of the type of blessing that the Lord is pouring over your life. It is a blessing that will not only minister to all of your needs and wants, but it will be too much in such a manner that it will overflow. Have you ever seen the riverbank that is full of water, when the water is too much it will overflow? That is what the Bible is trying to tell us in the book of Psalm 23. When you have feasted in the table of the Lord that he has set before your enemies, your cup is going to run over. The question is, what do you do with an overflowing cup? If the Lord has poured his blessings over your life and it is running over, what do you do with the overflow of the blessings? That is an important question because I do not believe that the Lord will want us to have everything overflowing without touching the lives of others around us.

Any time God gives you excess of what you ask for or require, the overflow or the excess is not yours. It is meant to touch the lives of other people. If you do not have this understanding, and your cup begins to run over, you will consume it upon yourself alone. God told

Abraham that, I will bless you so that you will also be a blessing.

Genesis 12:2

> *And I will make of thee a great*
> *nation, and I will bless thee, and*
> *make thy name great; and thou*
> *shalt be a blessing*

God will never fill our cups to overflow for ourselves alone or our families. There are people around us that have to be touched by what God has graciously given to us.

Friends, the reason why no life could be sustained in the Dead Sea is that the Dead Sea is always receiving, but never giving out. Water from the Sea of Galilee and other adjoining rivers flow into the Dead Sea, but the Dead Sea has no outlet to give out what it has been receiving over centuries. As a result of that, no life can be found there. It is completely dead without anything in it. I pray that the Lord will help us in the name of Jesus.

Scripture for Meditation

Psalm 16:5

> *The Lord is the portion of mine inheritance and of my cup: thou maintainest my lot.*

Reflection

Psalm 104:15

> *And wine that maketh glad the heart of man, and oil to make his face to shine, and bread which strengtheneth man's heart.*

Isaiah 25:6

> *And in this mountain shall the Lord of hosts make unto all people a feast of fat things, a*

*feast of wines on the lees, of fat
things full of marrow, of wines
on the lees well refined.*

Thank You Holy Father for the overrunning cup that you have bestowed upon my life to you be all the glory and the honour in the name of Jesus.

Holy Father, I make demands for the activation of the power of that Scripture in my life in the name of Jesus.

Heavenly Father, let the manifestation of the book of Psalms 23:5 become evident to all around my life in the name of Jesus.

Gracious Father, as my cup, begins to run over, help me not to be a reservoir alone but also a channel of the blessings that you have conferred upon my life in the name of Jesus.

Holy Father, deliver me from greed that will make me hold everything to myself and not use it to reach out to others that you have sent into my life in the name of Jesus.

Righteous Father, enlarge my mind to begin to see that the cup you have made to run over in my life is not only for me but to serve as a blessing to my country, and my generation in the name of Jesus.

Holy Father, let this cup of the blessing that you have placed on my life become a tool for bringing people into your kingdom in the name of Jesus.

Gracious Father, let the overflowing cup become a tool that will serve as a blessing to the body of Christ in the name of Jesus.

Thank You Holy Father for hearing and answering my prayers, to you be all the glory and the honour in the name of Jesus.

CHAPTER 13

Psalm 23:6

> *Surely goodness and mercy
> shall follow me all the days of
> my life:*

Goodness and Mercies

This is a great dimension of the shepherd that God is trying to portray to us. As long as we are his sheep, goodness and mercy will continue to pursue us. I want to explain what this goodness and mercy mean.

Goodness

The goodness of God is what gives the believer the privilege of experiencing some dimensions of God he had never seen. When Moses was leading the people of Israel out of the land of Egypt, he experienced a portion of the goodness of God. It was the goodness of God that caused Moses to enjoy the favour of seeing God more than the way the Israelites did.

Exodus 33:19

> *And he said, I will make all my goodness pass before thee, and I will proclaim the name of the Lord before thee; and will be gracious to whom I will be gracious, and will shew mercy on whom I will shew mercy.*

So the goodness of God is the favour that God gives to all of his children. It was as a result of the favour that Moses enjoyed before the Lord that made him see a dimension of God that was inaccessible to the children of Israel. It got to a point that God was showing Moses his ways, but the children of Israelites saw the acts of God. That is the goodness of God. The Bible tells us that in the book of Psalms 12:5, the Lord will surround the righteous with favour as a shield.

Mercies

Whenever we talk about the mercies of God, the first thing that some believers think of is the forgiveness of sins. That may be a part of it, but that's not all of it.

The mercies of God is what qualifies a believer to have things which ordinarily he can't have access to by human calculation. Throughout the Bible, we saw the mercies of God lifting people from where they are, to the place where God wants them to be. If not for the mercies of God, it won't have been possible for an orphan girl to become a Queen in a foreign land. It was the mercies of God that took Joseph, a prisoner, to the Palace as the vice president of Egypt. These are impossibilities to the human mind. But the mercies of God took these people to where they do not deserve to be. And if you can believe in the mercies of God, it will put you in position and places where your human abilities cannot take you.

I pray that the mercies and goodness of God will rest upon us in the name of Jesus.

Scripture for Meditation

Psalm 103:17

> *17 But the mercy of the Lord is from everlasting to everlasting upon them that fear him, and his righteousness unto children's children;*

Reflection

Psalm 36:7-11

How excellent is thy lovingkindness, O God! therefore the children of men put their trust under the shadow of thy wings.

8 They shall be abundantly satisfied with the fatness of thy house; and thou shalt make them drink of the river of thy pleasures.

9 For with thee is the fountain of life: in thy light shall we see light.

10 O continue thy lovingkindness unto them that know thee; and thy righteousness to the upright in heart.

11 Let not the foot of pride come against me, and let not the hand of the wicked remove me.

Psalm 17:15

As for me, I will behold thy face in righteousness: I shall be satisfied, when I awake, with thy likeness.

Thank You Holy Father for your goodness and mercies which you have bestowed upon me to you be all the glory and the honour in the name of Jesus.

Holy Father, in the same way, that you cause your goodness and your mercies to be manifested to Moses, I pray that you will cause that same goodness and mercies to encounter my life today in the name of Jesus.

Holy Father, let your goodness and mercies give me opportunities and privileges that are beyond my human capacity in the name of Jesus.

Heavenly Father, you have said in your word that your goodness and mercies will follow me. I pray that your goodness and your mercies will continue to pursue me everywhere I go in the name of Jesus.

Gracious Father, the same goodness and mercies you showed to Esther and Joseph, show it to me today in the name of Jesus.

Righteous Father, I pray that your favour will surround me in every dimension in my life in the name of Jesus.

Holy Father, I pray that let the privileges of being the sheep of the shepherd cause me to continue to enjoy your goodness and mercies forever in the name of Jesus.

Thank you holy father for hearing and answering my prayers, in the name of Jesus.

Pius **Joseph**

CHAPTER 14

Psalm 23:6

> *and I will dwell in the house of*
> *the Lord for ever.*

Dwelling in the House of the Lord

The concluding aspect of this Psalm reflects the
end of every believer. Our journey may have
started on earth, it is not permitted to end here.
The ultimate goal is to get into eternity with
Jesus forever. Which is why the Psalmist said, I
will dwell in the house of the Lord forever and
ever.

When Jesus was about to conclude his ministry on the earth, he told the disciples that he was going to prepare a place for them so that at the end of their work, they would come and join him. He said, in my father's house there are many mansions. So the dwelling in the house of the Lord that the Psalmist referred to, is for you to be in eternity with the Lord forever. If the goal of every believer is to die and go to the grave and everything ends there, we would have been of all men most miserable. Of course, the usual counsel will have been to eat and drink and when our life is over, we just die and go to the grave. But that is not the intent of God when he's dealing with his children.

There is a life beyond this life. If it wasn't so, God won't have said, precious in the sight of the Lord is the death of the saint. Which is the reason why as believers in Jesus Christ, we are to live our lives carefully believing that we have a home that is beyond this earth. And God intends to bring us to this place of eternal bliss.

Eternity has no time limitation. The Psalmist said it is forever and ever. Adam and Eve, Peter, Paul the apostle, and several other saints of old who have passed on to glory and have been in eternity for a very long time cannot exhaust eternal ages. The Bible tells us that one day is like a thousand years, and a thousand years is like a day before the Lord.

Psalm 91:7

> *A thousand shall fall at thy side, and ten thousand at thy right hand; but it shall not come nigh thee.*

The way time goes in eternity, is not the same way we calculate our time here on earth. May the Lord help us to walk righteously before him and dwell in his house forever and ever. Amen.

Scripture for Meditation

Psalms 21:4

He asked life of thee, and thou gavest it him, even length of days for ever and ever.

Reflection

Psalm 27:4

One thing have I desired of the Lord, that will I seek after; that I may dwell in the house of the Lord all the days of my life, to behold the beauty of the Lord, and to inquire in his temple.

2 Corinthians 5:1

For we know that if our earthly house of this tabernacle were dissolved, we have a building of God, an house not made with hands, eternal in the heavens.

Prayers

Thank You Holy Father for the assurance of your word that I will dwell in the house of the Lord for ever and ever. To you be all the glory and honour in the name of Jesus.

Holy Father, help me to walk with this consciousness that this earth isn't my home, but that you will want me to dwell in heaven forever in the name of Jesus.

Heavenly Father, every lifestyle that I am living right now that is capable of preventing me from enjoying the blessedness of the book of Psalm 23:6, of dwelling in your house forever, I ask that you help me to overcome it in the name of Jesus.

Righteous Father, help me to set my eyes on things above and not on things below in the name of Jesus.

Gracious Father, anything that is currently serving as a distraction to my journey towards dwelling in your house forever and ever, I ask that let that distraction be removed in the name of Jesus.

Holy Father, baptise me with the grace and the ability to live a life of righteousness and purity before you in the name of Jesus.

Righteous Father, you have said in your word that blessed are the pure in heart for they shall see God. I receive the grace of the purity of heart in the name of Jesus.

Thank you Holy Father for hearing and answering all of my prayers concerning the Psalms to you be all the glory and the honour in the name of Jesus.

Important Decision

If you are reading this book and you are not saved, pray this prayer after me:

Lord Jesus, I come before you today. I give you my heart. I give you my all. Come into my life. Become my Lord and saviour. Deliver me from the power of sin. Help me to live for you forever, in Jesus name.

Our Books

1.   Courtroom Prayers for Beginners: A Complete Guide to Courts of Heaven Prayers

2.   7 Powerful Prayers of Friendship with the Holy Spirit

3.   Restraining Decrees through Courtroom Prayers: Courts of Heaven Orders for Victory & Breakthroughs

4.   Python Spirit: Complete Deliverance from the Python Spirit with Powerful Prayers

25. How to Build a Life of Personal Devotion to God (Free-EBook)

26. The Holy Spirit Friendship Manual: How to make the Holy Ghost Your Close Friend (Free-EBook)

27. Walking in the Path of Divine Direction Always

28. The Expediency of Tongues

29. Breaking Soul Ties the Simple Way: How to Break Soul Ties and Receive Freedom

30. How to Read the Bible And Understand It

31. BAPTISM OF THE HOLY SPIRIT: Easy Steps to be Filled With the Holy Spirit And Obtain the Gifts of the Holy Spirit

32. Prayer That Never Fails

33. Vision from The Heavenly

34.   Baptism of the Holy Ghost Prayer Book: How to Minister the Baptism of the Holy Ghost to yourself and others.

35.   How to Hear God's Voice: A Believer's Manual For Talking with God

36.   Guide to Effective Fasting and Praying: A Way of Fasting And Prayers That Guarantee Results

Printed in Great Britain
by Amazon